VIETNAM WAR

# THE ORIGINS OF CONFLICT IN THE VIETNAM WAR

## VIETNAM WAR

# THE ORIGINS OF CONFLICT IN THE VIETNAM WAR

MASON CREST

Mason Crest
450 Parkway Drive, Suite D
Broomall, PA 19008
www.masoncrest.com

Cataloging-in-Publication Data on file with the Library of Congress.

Printed and bound in the United States of America.

First printing
9 8 7 6 5 4 3 2 1

ISBN: 978-1-4222-3888-2
Series ISBN: 978-1-4222-3887-5
ebook ISBN: 978-1-4222-7898-7
ebook series ISBN: 978-1-4222-7897-0

Produced by Regency House Publishing Limited
The Manor House
High Street
Buntingford
Hertfordshire
SG9 9AB
United Kingdom

www.regencyhousepublishing.com

Text copyright © 2018 Regency House Publishing Limited/Christopher Chant.

**PAGE 2:** Private First Class Russell R. Widdifield of 3rd Platoon, Company M, 3rd Battalion, 7th Marine Regiment, takes a break during a ground movement 25 miles north of An Hoa, North Vietnam.

**PAGE 3**: A U.S. Air Force Fairchild AC-119G Shadow from the 17th Special Operations Squadron from Nha Trang Air Base over Tan Son Nhut Air Base in 1969.

**RIGHT:** Second Lieutenant Kathleen M. Sullivan treats a Vietnamese child during Operation MED CAP, a U.S. Air Force civic action program in which a team of .doctors, nurses, and aides travel to Vietnamese villages, treat the sick and teach villagers the basics of sanitation and cleanliness.

**PAGE 6**: Protests against the war in Washington, D.C. on April 24, 1971.

TITLES IN THE VIETNAM WAR SERIES:

**The Origins of Conflict in the Vietnam War**
**The Escalation of American Involvement in the Vietnam War**
**The U.S. Ground War in Vietnam 1965–1973**
**Stalemate: U.S. Public Opinion of the War in Vietnam**
**The Fall of Saigon and the End of the Vietnam War**

# CONTENTS

# KEY ICONS TO LOOK FOR:

 **Words to Understand:** These words with their easy-to-understand definitions will increase the reader's understanding of the text, while building vocabulary skills.

 **Sidebars:** This boxed material within the main text allows readers to build knowledge, gain insights, explore possibilities, and broaden their perspectives by weaving together additional information to provide realistic and holistic perspectives.

 **Educational Videos:** Readers can view videos by scanning our QR codes, providing them with additional content to supplement the text. Examples include news coverage, moments in history, speeches, iconic sports moments, and much more!

 **Text-Dependent Questions:** These questions send the reader back to the text for more careful attention to the evidence presented here.

 **Research Projects:** Readers are pointed toward areas of further inquiry connected to each chapter. Suggestions are provided for projects that encourage deeper research and analysis.

 **Series Glossary of Key Terms:** This back-of-the-book glossary contains terminology used throughout the series. Words found here increase the reader's ability to read and comprehend high-level books and articles in this field.

**OPPOSITE**: A UH-1D Medevac helicopter takes off to pick up an injured member of the 101st Airborne Division in South Vietnam.

# Vietnam Veterans Memorial

The Vietnam Veterans Memorial was designed by Maya Lin, a 21-year-old from Athens, Ohio. It was unveiled with an opening ceremony in 1982 in Washington, D.C.

The memorial is dedicated to the men and women in the U.S. military who served in the war zone of Vietnam. The names of the 58,000 Americans who gave their lives and service to their country are etched chronologically in gabbro stone and listed on the two walls which make up the memorial monument. Those who died in action are denoted by a diamond, those who were missing (MIAs, POWs, and others) are denoted with a cross. When the death of one, who was previously missing is confirmed, a diamond is superimposed over a cross.

The wall consists of two sections, one side points to the Lincoln Memorial and the other to the Washington Monument. There is a pathway along the base for visitors to walk and reflect, or view the names of their loved ones.

When visiting the memorial many take a piece of paper, and using a crayon or soft pencil make a memento of their loved one. This is known as "rubbing." The shiny wall was designed to reflect a visitor's face while reading the names of the military personnel who lost their lives. The idea is that symbolically the past and present are represented. The memorial was paid for by the Vietnam Veterans Memorial Fund, Inc. who raised nearly $9,000,000 to complete it.

The memorial site also includes The Three Servicemen statue built in 1984. The statue depicts three soldiers, purposefully identifiable as *European American, African American,* and *Hispanic American.* The statue faces the wall with the soldiers looking on in solemn tribute at the names of their fallen comrades.

The Vietnam Women's Memorial is dedicated to the women of the United States who served in the Vietnam War, most of whom were nurses. It serves as a reminder of the importance of women in the conflict.

The Vietnam Veterans Memorial can be found to the north of the Lincoln Memorial near the intersection of 22nd St. and Constitution Ave. NW. The memorial is maintained by the U.S. National Park Service, and receives approximately 5 million visitors each year. It is open 24 hours a day and is free to all visitors.

## Chapter One
# A LONG LEGACY

Also known as the Second Indochina War and the U.S. War in Vietnam, the Vietnam War lasted from 1965 to the Communist victory on April 30, 1975, but is sometimes dated to a start in 1959. Of the several other names associated with this conflict, the one most generally used is the Vietnam War. It is worth noting, however, that the appellation Second Indochina War is useful in contextualizing the conflict in relation to the First Indochina War that resulted in the departure of the French as the colonial power, and linking the Vietnam War with the other conflicts being fought in South-

East Asia at various times during this period: thus Vietnam, Laos, and Cambodia can be seen as the theaters

in which a larger Indochinese conflict was fought, between the end of the Second World War in 1945 and the Communist victory in 1975.

The term Vietnam Conflict is used primarily in the USA to indicate that Congress never formally declared war on North Vietnam, and that in purely legal terms the president made use of his constitutionally mandated authority, on many occasions supplemented by resolutions in the Congress, to have the U.S. forces fight what was described as a "police action."

## Words to Understand

**Defoliant:** Chemicals applied to plants causing their leaves to drop off, often to remove cover from an enemy in war.

**Guerrilla:** A person who engages in irregular warfare, harassing the enemy by sabotage or surprise raids.

**Indochina:** Peninsula in south-eastern Asia comprising six countries.

**LEFT:** Vietnam 1949. The French position is overrun by the Vietnamese after a five-hour fight during the Battle of Pho Rang in north-eastern Vietnam.

**OPPOSITE ABOVE:** French troops at the commencement of insurgent action in the Tonkin area in 1947.

**OPPOSITE BELOW:** French armored troops clearing countryside near Saigon in October 1945.

increasingly open warfare. The Vietnam War was the first major military defeat suffered by the United States of America, and as such was a very considerable psychological and emotional blow to a nation accustomed to success, but already socially and culturally riven by the anti-war movement, in the media as well as among major segments of the American population, which had played such a significant part in undermining the resolve of the American forces in South-East Asia.

Something in the order of 1.4 million military personnel, about one in 17 of them American, lost their lives in the war, and civilian deaths have been estimated variously as between 2 and 5 million or slightly more for the two Vietnams, to which have to be added up to 700,000 Cambodian and 50,000 Laotian civilians. The war was fought between the Democratic Republic of Vietnam,

The term Vietnam War is that which is most generally used in the English-speaking world, but falsely suggests that it was fought wholly inside the two Vietnams, and so tacitly ignores the fact that the conflict spilled over into Cambodia and Laos.

Finally, the term most generally used in North Vietnam, and in the unified country until recent times, is the Resistance War against the Americans to Save the Nation. This is more a propaganda slogan than a real name, and in many ways mirrors the USSR's use of the term Great Patriotic War to describe its part in the Second World War.

On the final day of the war, the Communist forces under North Vietnamese leadership took Saigon, the capital of South Vietnam, even as the last U.S. forces were being pulled out by air to vessels awaiting offshore, sealing the North Vietnamese military victory after more than 15 years of

generally known as North Vietnam, and the Republic of Vietnam, known as South Vietnam. The latter was supported by the USA and, at various times, by other allies, which supplied men and equipment in varying numbers and types. The Communist triumph led to South Vietnam's absorption by North Vietnam into the creation of a single Communist state.

The USA and other South Vietnamese allies sent large numbers of troops to South Vietnam between the end of the First Indochina War in 1954 and 1973. U.S. military advisers made their first appearance in Vietnam during 1950 to aid the French forces seeking to secure colonial rule in this part of Indo-China. They took over the complete task of training the Army of the Republic of Vietnam, generally abbreviated as the ARVN, during 1956. From this time forward there was a steady increase in the attempts of Communist elements, under the control of the North Vietnamese, to subvert the pro-Western government and administration of South Vietnam, and this led to a steady escalation of

**OPPOSITE:** British and French troops engaged in clearing the Saigon triangle in October 1945.

**RIGHT:** French troops in 1952.

**BELOW:** A Grumman F8F Bearcat ground crew lift bomb to wing.

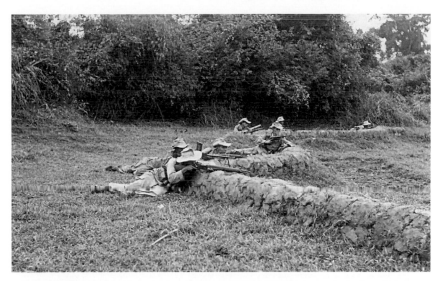

the USA's support for South Vietnam. During his presidency, John F. Kennedy authorized the increase in U.S. troop numbers in South Vietnam from 500 to 16,000, and this process was taken considerably further from

**LEFT:** A convoy moving out to the countryside with Japanese troops in October 1945.

**BELOW:** July 1950, when French troops became involved with the Communists in South Vietnam between Ba Ria and Cap St. Jacques. Here a Viet Minh (Communist) prisoner has been frisked by two French soldiers, one of whom is examining the flag bearing the hammer and sickle symbol found on the boy.

U.S. Air Force and U.S. Navy, complemented by machines of the U.S. Army, undertook major air support of the forces fighting the "in-country" war, and also launched huge bombing programs directed at the

1965 by Kennedy's successor as president, Lyndon B. Johnson. The numbers of US troops were reduced steadily from the early 1960s as the USA attempted to "Vietnamize" the anti-Communist effort, and nearly all of the U.S. military personnel departed South Vietnam after the Paris Peace Accords of 1973, the last of them leaving on April 30, 1975 in Operation Frequent Wind, as the Communists moved into Saigon.

The war was extremely varied in its nature, as dictated by the course of events, the terrain over which the war was being fought, and the nature of the forces involved. The war therefore included small-scale fighting between minor units moving through the mountains and jungles, amphibious and airborne operations of different sizes, Communist guerrilla attacks on villages and urban areas, and major land battles of a conventional nature operating from land bases as well as aircraft carriers maneuvering off the east coast of Vietnam. Aircraft of the

**ABOVE:** Digging in after taking over a sector from the Vietnamese rebels in Indo-China. Franco-Vietnam troops are shown standing knee-deep in water and keeping their firearms leveled at the rebel troops who are a short distance away. Note the leader of the group using a portable radio to contact the head of his sector.

industrics, logistical systems (especially railway, road, river, and canal networks), urban centers and ports of North Vietnam. Other aspects of the Vietnam War, which should not be ignored or belittled, are that Cambodia and Laos were also drawn into the conflict, and that the Americans sprayed very large quantities of chemicals onto the land from the air in an effort to reduce the amount of natural cover available to their foe. This use of **defoliant** agents marked the emergence of a new form of warfare, and has had a long-term effect on large parts of Vietnam and on the health of many Vietnamese.

For most of the period between 110 BC and AD 938, a large part of what is now Vietnam was part of China. After gaining independence, Vietnam had to fight hard and long to retain this independence in the face of foreign aggression and internal conflict over many centuries between the Trinh and Nguyen lords. The latter ended only in 1802, when the Emperor Gia Long unified modern Vietnam under the Nguyen dynasty. Between 1859 and 1885, however, the French gained control of Indo-China (Cambodia, Laos, and Vietnam) in the course of colonial wars. Indochinese laborers were important to the French war effort in the First World War (1914–18), and at the Versailles Conference of 1919, which led to the Treaty of Versailles ending the war between Germany and the allies, Ho Chi Minh ("the Enlightener") requested that a Vietnamese delegation be involved as an element of Vietnam's search for independence from French rule. Ho hoped it would catch the attention of the U.S. president, Woodrow Wilson, who was a strong believer in the concept of

national self-determination. Wilson refused to be drawn, but the Vietnamese cause was taken up by elements of the French left.

In the Second World War (1939–45), the authorities of Vichy France, the state which controlled that part of France left unoccupied by the Germans after the Franco-German armistice of June 1940, lacked the strength at home or abroad to resist the political and military pressure exerted by an expansionist Japanese empire, and came to cooperate with the Japanese forces which entered Indochina and established garrisons and bases there. Thus Vietnam came to be under the practical control of Japan, even though the latter was

content to leave the French administration to run the colony.

It was during 1941 that a Communist-dominated national resistance group, the League for the Independence of Vietnam, more generally known as the Viet Minh, came into existence, quickly falling under the domination of Ho Chi Minh after his return to Vietnam. Ho had been a Comintern agent since the 1920s, but as the leader of an independent Vietnamese Communist party, he was now increasingly separating himself from Soviet influences and control while prudently maintaining good relations with the Soviets. Under Ho's leadership, the Viet Minh began to develop and refine

**ABOVE:** Peasants assisting the Viet Minh in the north of Vietnam in 1951.

**OPPOSITE:** The tank played a very important role throughout the entire Vietnam War.

a political and military strategy to seize control of the country at the end of the war, after the Japanese had been defeated by the allies, and appointed Vo Nguyen Giap as commander of the movement's clandestine military branch.

With a view to securing external aid for his movement, whose longer-term and real objectives remained veiled in secrecy, Ho used the guerrilla forces under Giap's supervision to make attacks on the Japanese. This persuaded the Americans, in the form of the Office of Strategic Services, which was the precursor of the Central Intelligence Agency, to provide funding and training. The Viet Minh guerrilla forces maintained a low-key campaign against the Japanese in Indochina, and also aided other indigenous resistance groups. The Viet Minh effort was not all a blind, however, for it was able to provide the allies with important intelligence on Japanese troop movements, and also effected the recovery and succour of many of the crews of American warplanes that had been brought down in Indochina. In overall terms, however, the USA believed the only correct strategy was to strike straight at the heart of the enemy's military and political strength, using the most direct course available. This suggested that the Americans saw the efforts of the Viet Minh in Indochina as nothing more than a sideshow which might inconvenience the Japanese slightly, and should therefore be supported at only the most minimal level.

In 1944 the Japanese saw the possible advantage of a major change of tack in their grasp of Indochina, and thus overthrew the Vichy French administration, while also subjecting its officials to humiliation in front of the Vietnamese population. Both aspects of the end of Vichy French rule had major repercussions within Indochina, for they provided real

**LEFT:** Troops on Cap St. Jacques in September 1945.

**BELOW:** The *Bois Belleau* light aircraft carrier arrives in the Gulf of Tonkin in 1954.

**OPPOSITE:** European residents of Hanoi welcome French troops in March 1946.

groupings within Vietnam, some nationalist, others Communist, and still others not overtly political in being aligned with neither of the major power blocs of the period, felt that they had every opportunity to seize control of Vietnam. In the event, the surrendering Japanese army transferred the reins of power to the Viet Minh, and the Emperor Bao Dai abdicated. On September 2, 1945 Ho declared Vietnamese independence from France in the so-called "August Revolution." It all seemed so clear-cut that U.S. Army officers stood beside Ho on the platform, in front of a great audience in Hanoi, as the Viet Minh leader launched himself into a speech using the American Declaration of

proof that both the administration and personnel of a European power were just as vulnerable as they were themselves, and that independence, therefore, was not merely a pipe dream, but something they could work toward with a very real chance of success.

The Japanese also began to encourage the growth of nationalism, and made the shrewd political move of granting Vietnam independence, even though this was nominal rather than real. On March 11, 1945 the Emperor Bao Dai declared the independence of Vietnam within what the Japanese were pleased to call their Greater East Asia Co-Prosperity Sphere.

In the aftermath of the Japanese surrender in August 1945, various

an indigenous nationalist movement, despite the fact that it was of Communist ideology. Ho's hopes had been raised in this respect by a number of wartime speeches by President Franklin D. Roosevelt, opposing any return of European powers to their pre-war colonial empires. Ho also went as far as to tell a representative of the OSS that Vietnam would have "a million American soldiers…but no French." At this juncture, however, the anti-colonial feeling evident in the USA since its emergence as a nation in the War of American Independence (1775–83) succumbed to realpolitik. The American reasoning was simple: it was now clear that France could and should be a key player in U.S.-led efforts to deter, and if necessary fight off the Soviet territorial ambitions in continental Europe, and that France's colonial ambitions were something that had to be factored into the equation.

The new Viet Minh government survived for only the briefest of periods. At the Potsdam Conference, which ended on August 2, 1945, the allies had decided that Vietnam should be occupied, on a temporarily basis, by British and Chinese forces, which would accept the surrender of the Japanese troops in the country, disarm them, and begin the process of repatriating them to Japan. The first Chinese troops appeared in northern Vietnam only a few days after Ho's declaration of independence, and the Viet Minh government thereupon went out of existence as a practical reality. The Chinese then seized control of the area of Vietnam north of the 16th parallel, the first British forces arriving in the area south of this *de facto* dividing line, where they began to take control from the dispirited Japanese, so restoring a measure of order in a region that had grown increasingly lawless. Admiral

Vietnam forces in Indochina found that commando warfare in small bands was the most effective fighting method in wiping out the marauding and pillaging Viet Minh guerrilla bands infesting Tonkin. Here Indochinese commandos are searching a fortified village in Tonkin. They must proceed with extreme caution because of the traps and hidden grenades that are planted everywhere.

Independence as one of its models: "All men are created equal. They are endowed by their Creator with certain inalienable rights; among these are Life, Liberty, and the pursuit of Happiness." This immortal statement was made in the Declaration of Independence of the United States of America in 1776… We…solemnly declare to the world that Vietnam has the right to be a free and independent country. The entire Vietnamese people are determined…to sacrifice their lives and property in order to safeguard their independence and liberty.'

In this manner Ho hoped to secure U.S. approval for the assumption of power in Vietnam by

Lord Louis Mountbatten, the British commander-in-chief of the Allies' South-East Asia Command, moved more than 20,000 men of Major General D. Gracey's Indian 20th

**OPPOSITE:** Vietnamese Republican soldiers are seen entering a burning village in Indochina during fighting with French forces.

**ABOVE:** French troops, still wearing U.S.-supplied uniforms, depart from Marseilles to reinforce French forces in the Indo-Chinese conflict in September

Infantry Division in to occupy Saigon. The first of the men reached the major city of southern Vietnam on September 6, and the rest of the British-led Indian force arrived during the next few weeks, but were so overstretched that they had to rearm a number of Japanese prisoners-of-war to create the so-called Gremlin Force to aid them in less hard-pressed areas. The British began to withdraw from southern Vietnam during December 1945, but did not complete the bulk of this process until May 1946. The last British casualties in Vietnam were suffered in June 1946. Altogether 40 British and Indian troops were killed

and over 100 were wounded. Vietnamese casualties were 600.

As the Anglo-Indian forces pulled out, the first elements of the returning French arrived, the French authorities immediately attempting to gain control of the situation in the north as well as the south of Vietnam. The French negotiated with the Chinese nationalist forces of Generalissimo Chiang Kai-shek, agreeing to end French treaty concessions in China in exchange for Chinese authorization for a French return to northern Vietnam, so that they could start direct negotiation with the Viet Minh. Ho was just as enthusiastic about the

**ABOVE:** Operation Artois, January 1953. An important clean-up operation began on January 16 to the north-east and east of Thai Binh after serious combats at Lang Dong on the 20th and at An Trach and Lai Tri on the 21st and 22nd, in which 328 Viet Minh were killed and 183 prisoners and numerous armaments were taken by the French forces.

**LEFT:** Communist troops move to take Haiphong.

**OPPOSITE ABOVE:** Vietnam 1953. A group of captured French officers after the fight for Nghia Lo. First on the left is the French area commander of Nghia Lo.

possibilities attached to a Chinese withdrawal, and took advantage of the interregnum to kill as many as possible of the leaders and members of rival nationalist groupings.

Talks concerning the formation of a Vietnamese government within the new, all-embracing French Union ended in failure, and the French attempted to exert pressure with a bombardment of Haiphong, the major port lying close to Hanoi. In December 1946 the French occupied Hanoi, and the Americans studiously ignored a number of telegrams from Ho, asking for President Harry S. Truman's political support. In the

short term, therefore, Ho decided that he and the surviving cadres of the Viet Minh would make a fall-back into the inhospitable mountains of north-western Vietnam to prepare and launch an armed insurgency.

This marked the beginning of the First Indochina War (1946–54), which was to be both long and bloody, the military losses of the French and their allies, at 94,581 dead, 78,127 wounded, and 40,000 taken prisoner, being greater than the USA would suffer during the Vietnam War. The Communist losses in the First Indochina War would also be considerable, being in the order of

more than 300,000 dead, more than 500,000 wounded, and about 100,000 taken prisoner.

It appears that the position of the USA vis-à-vis Indochina was indecisive during this period. On the one hand the USA, convinced that colonialism was wrong, wished to convince France to reconsider its position in Indochina but to leave the exact nature and timing of the process to France itself. During the Second World War, President Roosevelt had steadily stalled French demands for U.S. help in reclaiming Indochina, and after the end of the war the French agreed that

Battle of Dien Bien Phu

decolonialization was probably the right long-term course and that, in accordance with the principles of the newly created United Nations Organization, a measure of autonomy should be offered to Indochina, but only after France had managed to regain control of the region.

On the other hand, the USA had real concerns about Ho's allegiance, in world terms, following the Second World War, when it was clear that the two major power blocs would be those led by the USA and the USSR. In the eyes of the power players in Washington, however, every element in the world admitting or claiming to be Communist had to be in thrall to the leadership of the USSR, therefore it was inevitable that the USA, when asked by Ho for recognition of the Viet Minh government of northern Vietnam, should perceive Ho, not as a neutral Communist but as a man concealing his control by the USSR. This was an American perception which played into the hands of the French and, as U.S. Secretary of State Dean Acheson wrote, "...the U.S. came to the aid of the French... because we needed their support for our policies in regard to NATO...The French blackmailed us. At every meeting...they brought up Indochina...but refused to tell me what they hoped to accomplish or how. Perhaps they didn't know."

The First Indochina War, otherwise known as the French Indochina War, Franco-Vietnamese War, Franco-Viet Minh War, Indochina War, and Dirty War in France, and as the French War in Vietnam, lasted from December 19, 1946 to August 1, 1954, and was fought between the Far East Expeditionary Corps of the French Union, with the support of Bao Dai's Vietnamese National Army, and the Viet Minh led by Ho Chi Minh and Vo Nguyen Giap.

Most of the fighting took place in the Tonkin region of northern Vietnam, although parts of the war spread to other parts of the country, as well as to the neighboring protectorates of Laos and Cambodia within the French Indochinese empire.

**OPPOSITE:** The victorious Vietnamese enter Hanoi in October 1954.

**ABOVE:** A French artillery position at Dien Bien Phu.

**RIGHT:** Members of the planning section at Viet Minh GHQ discuss future tactics.

**OPPOSITE:** French military police watch the red flag go up over Haiphong.

**ABOVE:** French troops at a water crossing.

The war began as a rebellion launched by the Viet Minh against the French authorities controlling Indochina. The first few years of the war took the form of a low-intensity rural insurgency against French authority, but once the Chinese Communist forces had advanced against the Chinese nationalist forces to the border of Vietnam and China during 1949, the scale and intensity of the conflict escalated sharply into conventional war between two armies equipped with modern weapons supplied by the two superpower blocs.

The forces of the French Union not only included troops from France's former colonies of Algeria, Cambodia, Laos, Morocco, Tunis, and Vietnam, but also those from West and Central Africa, together with the professionals of the French Foreign Legion. The use of troops from metropolitan France was prohibited by the government in an effort to avoid unpopularity at home, but even so the level of antipathy to the war effort rose steadily, not only because of the cost, but also through the effort of left-wing elements, who called this the *sale guerre* (dirty war).

While the strategy of drawing the Viet Minh to attack well-defended bases in the remoter parts of the country at the extreme end of the Communist forces' logistical capability was essentially sound, and achieved very useful results in the Battle of Na San, a truly effective defense of French interests was impossible for lack of materials

(especially concrete) with which to build the defenses, of armored fighting vehicles for lack of surface access, and of the air cover that would otherwise have exercised a dominant effect. Therefore the French were gradually being driven to a major and totally exhausting defeat, with significant losses among their most mobile troops.

General Philippe Leclerc de Hauteclocque had reached Saigon on October 9, 1945 in company with Colonel Jacques Émile Massu's Groupement de Marche. Leclerc's primary tasks were defined as the restoration of public order in southern Vietnam and the militarization of the Tonkin region of northern Vietnam, while his secondary tasks were the holding of the current position while awaiting the advent of more French forces with which to retake Chinese-occupied Hanoi, and then the undertaking of negotiations with the Viet Minh.

The war proper began in Haiphong after disagreement concerning the level of import duty on goods arriving at the port, and on November 23, 1946 French warships bombarded the city and, according to differing sources, in the process killed somewhere between 2,000 and more than 6,000 Vietnamese civilians in the single afternoon. The bombardment's positive effect, if that is the right way to describe it, was to persuade the Viet Minh to agree to a cease-fire and

**ABOVE:** French prisoners taken after the Battle of Dien Bien Phu.

**OPPOSITE:** Franco-Vietnamese soldiers, supported by tanks, move forward under fire for a counterattack on March 23, 1954 against the rebel Viet Minh forces around the besieged fortress of Dien Bien Phu. The action resulted in the obliteration of a complete Viet Minh company at a point south of the post.

to depart from Haiphong. The Viet Minh saw this as a tactical reverse rather than a major defeat, however, and Vo Nguyen Giap soon brought up 30,000 men to attack Haiphong. The French were outnumbered but had better weapons and the advantages of heavy fire support from their warships, and this made it impossible for the Viet Minh to consider any form of frontal assault. By December, fighting had also erupted in Hanoi, and Ho was forced to leave the city and fall back into remote mountain areas relatively inaccessible to the French. This marked the stage at which guerrilla warfare became the standard way of waging the war, with the French in control of almost all apart from the most extremely remote of areas.

In 1946 Vo Nguyen Giap moved his headquarters to Tan Trao. The French tried to reach and attack his main centres of strength, but on every occasion Giap refused to be drawn into combat with superior strength and maneuvered his forces out of the way: thus it became a standard Viet Minh tactic to disappear as the French approached. Late in 1947 the French undertook Operation Lea to take and destroy the Viet Minh communications nexus at Bac Kan, but failed to capture Giap and his senior subordinates, which had also been part of the operation's objectives. They nonetheless were able to kill 9,000 Viet Minh soldiers in the course of the campaign, which can be regarded only as a major defeat for the Viet Minh.

In 1948 France saw the sense of opposing the Viet Minh politically as well as militarily, and established an alternative government in Saigon. Here the French began negotiations with Bao Dai, the former Vietnamese

emperor, to head an "autonomous" government of the State of Vietnam within the French Union. Two years before, the French had refused Ho's similar suggestion, but with a number of restrictions on French power and a political evolution toward France's eventual withdrawal from Vietnam. Now the French were prepared to offer a similar "deal" to Bao Dai as he had cooperated with the French in the past; lacking armed forces, Bao Dai was in no position to make any major objection, although he would be in possession of such forces in the near future.

In 1949 France officially recognized the State of Vietnam under Bao Dai as independent within the French Union. But this independence was only nominal, and then only within the French Union, as France kept control of matters related to foreign and military affairs. The Viet Minh immediately denounced the State of Vietnam as a puppet of the French, demanding real independence. As a concession to the new state and as a means of increasing the number of troops available to it for service in

**LEFT:** Operation Castor in 1953.

**ABOVE LEFT:** Paratroopers seize a Viet Minh base in Operation Castor. With his parachute still lying behind him, a paratrooper mans an automatic weapon during a Franco-Vietnamese parachute attack on Dien Bien Phu on November 20, 1953. Several thousand French Vietnamese dropped in the neighborhood, occupying the important Viet Minh base almost without resistance

**OPPOSITE:** A Viet Minh leaflet advising French defenders of Dien Bien Phu to surrender.

Vietnam, France sanctioned the establishment of a Vietnamese National Army with Vietnamese officers. Once the VNA had been created, its units were employed to garrison quiet sectors, freeing the French forces for serious combat. (The private armies of the Cao Dai, Hoa Hao, and Binh Xuyen criminal organizations were also used in the same manner.) In the same year, however, the Vietnamese Communists also began to receive outside aid, after Mao's Communist forces gained total control of China by defeating Chiang's Kuomintang forces, which decamped to Formosa (Taiwan). Thus the Viet Minh gained a significant supporter and source of supplies in an area just across the border from its stronghold area.

It should be noted that, in the same year, France additionally recognized the independence, again within the context of the French Union, of Cambodia and Laos, the other two kingdoms constituting the French empire in Indochina.

During 1950 the USA recognized the State of Vietnam but, even so, many other countries, even in the West, continued to regard it solely as a French creature. Part of the USA's new-found commitment to the region as its "new administration" took the form of weapons and military observers. On the other side of the "front," however, the Chinese were supplying effectively unlimited quantities of Soviet matériel to the Viet Minh, so that Giap was in the position to reconstitute his guerrilla and other irregular forces into five conventional formations, namely the 304th, 308th, 312th, 316th, and 320th Divisions. Strengthened and remodeled in this fashion, the Communist forces went over to the offensive, initially by attacking French bases effectively isolated along the Sino-Vietnamese border. In February

1950, Giap's forces overran the 150-strong French garrison at Lai Khe in the Tonkin region, just south of the border with China. Thereby encouraged, Giap next moved to Cao Bang, where on May 25 his forces attacked a garrison of 4,000 Vietnamese troops under French command but were repulsed. Giap again attacked Cao Bang, and also Dong Khe on September 15. Dong Khe fell to the Communist forces on September 18, and Cao Bang finally succumbed on October 3. Giap moved immediately against Lang Son, which was held by 4,000 men of the French Foreign Legion. Falling back along

Route 4, the legionnaires, and a relief force from That Khe, were ambushed along the length of their retreat by the Communist forces. The French dropped a paratroop battalion south of Dong Khe to draw off some of the Communist strength, but the battalion was cut off, surrounded and destroyed. On October 17, and after seven days of Communist attacks, Lang Son fell. By the time the last elements of their defeated garrisons had entered the relative safety of the Red river delta, the French had lost 4,800 men dead, missing or taken prisoner, as well as 2,000 men wounded out of a garrison strength of

more than 10,000. The French also lost 13 guns, 125 mortars, 450 trucks, 940 machine guns, 1,200 sub-machine guns, and 8,000 rifles.

Thus China and the USSR recognized the Viet Minh as the legitimate administration of Vietnam, and increased their flow of matériel and supplies.

In 1951 France began to detect a glimmer of distant light on the horizon when a new commander-in-chief, namely General Jean-Marie de Lattre de Tassigny, arrived to reconsider the problem of maintaining French rule. De Lattre ordered the construction of a fortified defense line, which became known as the De Lattre Line, between Hanoi and the Gulf of Tonkin via the Red river delta. De Lattre believed this line could be the fixed anvil against which his mobile force could shatter the Viet Minh, and initially his concept worked well.

The following January 13 saw Giap directing the 20,000 or more men of the 308th and 312th Divisions to attack Vinh Yen, which lies some 20 miles (32km) to the north-west of Hanoi, and which was held by the 6,000 men of the 9th Foreign Legion Brigade. The Viet Minh hurled themselves into a neatly conceived trap, when, caught in the open for the first time, the men of the Communist divisions were shot to pieces by concentrated French artillery and machine gun fire. By January 16 Giap was forced to admit defeat after losing more than 6,000 of his men killed,

**OPPOSITE:** French paratroops landing at Dien Bien Phu airfield.

**RIGHT:** Vietnamese refugees in a restaurant tent at La Pagoda wait for their "passage to freedom" in September 1954.

8,000 wounded, and 500 captured, and ordered a withdrawal. The Battle of Vinh Yen had been a disaster for the Communist cause in Vietnam, and the French now believed they possessed at least one tactical answer to the military problem of the Viet Minh.

On March 23 Giap made another move against the French, this time launching an attack against Mao Khe, lying some 20 miles (32km) north of Haiphong. The 11,000 troops of the 316th Division, with the partly rebuilt 308th and 312th Divisions in reserve, were held off and then repulsed in hand-to-hand fighting, the French defense effort supported by warplanes using napalm and rockets, and also by the guns of the French warships steaming along the coast. After losing 3,000 men dead and wounded, Giap ordered a withdrawal on March 28.

The Communist military commander was nothing if not dedicated, however, and on May 29 committed his forces to yet another offensive, in which the 304th Division moved against Phu Ly, the 308th Division moved against Ninh Binh and, as the main effort, the 320th Division moved against Phat Diem, lying to the south of Hanoi. This co-ordinated trio of efforts suffered just as badly as had the earlier offensives, and the three divisions suffered heavy casualties.

This was the ideal moment for the French to strike, and de Lattre launched a counteroffensive against the Viet Minh, which had suffered something of a failure of morale over the last period of fighting and was now driven back into the jungle, losing a number of outposts in the Red river

delta by June 18. The French counter-offensive cost the Viet Minh more than 10,000 more men killed.

Thus every one of Giap's attempts to break the De Lattre Line ended in defeat, and at the same time elicited a French counterattack inflicting heavy losses on the Viet Minh. The losses of Giap's forces had risen almost catastrophically in this period, when the still comparatively lightly equipped Viet Minh faced high-quality French troops in prepared positions with an abundance of heavy weapons and air power at their disposal. The reverses even persuaded some leading Vietnamese figures, including some in the party, to question the leadership of the Communist government. But while the military balance in Vietnam had been tipped in favor of the French, the political and social balance in France was tipping in the other direction as

**OPPOSITE:** French and Vietnamese forces launch a new attack against Viet Minh troops to the north of Dien Bien Phu on February 1 and 2, 1954.

**BELOW:** U.S.-supplied Douglas B-26 Invader attack warplanes, used in the Battle of Dien Bien Phu in March 1954.

opposition to the war increased. The financial cost to the French nation was high and increasing steadily, and while all of the French forces in Indo-China were professional soldiers rather than conscripts, there was great concern that officers were being killed at a rate greater than the training schools were generating replacements. The officer replacement factor was something which had to be resolved in France, but as far as the financial

aspect was concerned, France turned to the USA for support.

On November 14, 1951 the French initiated an airborne operation to seize Hoa Binh, which lay some 25 miles (40km) west of the De Lattre Line, and were thus able to deepen their perimeter defenses in this area. Inevitably, however, the Viet Minh counterattacked the expanded French position at Hoa Binh, forcing the French back to their original De Lattre

Line positions by February 22 of the following year. The losses of more than 10,000, split equally between the two sides, clearly indicated that the war was still far from over.

In January 1952 de Latte was invalided back to France with cancer, and died shortly after reaching his homeland. He was replaced as French Commander-in-Chief in Indochina by General Raoul Salan. Throughout 1952, and in most parts of northern Vietnam, the Viet Minh concentrated its efforts on severing the French lines of communication and supply, hoping to effect a serial erosion of the French forces' morale and resolve in the process. The Viet Minh launched an apparently never-ending sequence of raids, skirmishes, and guerrilla

attacks, but it was clear that this was not a decisive moment, and each side used the opportunity to prepare for larger operations.

On October 17 Giap committed a sizeable part of his strength to attacks on the French garrisons along the Nghia Lo, to the north-west of Hanoi, but broke off the attacks when the arrival of a French parachute battalion threatened his position. The Communist forces had control over most of the Tonkin region outside the De Lattre Line and Salan, perceiving this to be a critical moment, committed his forces in Operation Lorraine, along the Clear river, in an effort to compel Giap to lift the Communist pressure on the Nghia Lo outposts. This involved the greatest

**ABOVE:** General J. Lawton Collins, U.S. Army Chief of Staff (second from left) and General Jean de Lattre de Tassigny, High Commissioner of French Indochina (with armband), accompanied by local officials en route to address citizens of Hanoi at a welcoming ceremony given in honor of General Collins in 1951.

**OPPOSITE:** Members of the Vietnamese People's Army rejoicing after their victory at Dien Bien Phu in 1954.

French effort in Indochina up to that time, and began on October 29 as 30,000 French soldiers advanced from the De Lattre Line against the Communist supply dumps in the area of Phu Yen. The French took Phu Tho on November 5, Phu Doan on November 9, by means of an airborne operation, and finally Phu Yen on November 13. Giap did not react immediately to the French offensive, for he believed that it would be better to allow the more supply-dependent French to reach the end of their communication and supply capability before striking at these lines to cut the French off from their base area in the Red river delta. Salan was too astute to fall into this trap, however, and halted the operation on November 14, taking his forces back toward the De Lattre Line. The only major fighting during the operation came during the withdrawal, when the Viet Minh ambushed the French column at Chan

Muong on November 17. An Indochinese *bataillon de marche* cleared the Viet Minh block with a bayonet charge, and the withdrawal continued. The operation was thus only partially successful, but while it revealed the fact that the French could strike out at targets beyond the De Lattre line, such efforts did not cause the Viet Minh to call off its own offensive, or inflict significant damage on the Communist logistical system, which was altogether more diffuse than that of the French, in that it was not wholly reliant on the road, rail, and waterway systems of the area.

Giap used the winter of 1952–53 to reconsider his whole strategic approach to ousting the French from Indochina. He now realized that direct attacks on an enemy enjoying the benefits offered by fixed positions and heavier weapons cost lives and equipment to no good effect, and decided to exert pressure on the

French by opening another front. Thus on April 9 the Communist forces began to advance into Laos. During May, Salan was replaced as commander-in-chief of the French forces by General Henri Navarre, who signaled the French government that "there is no possibility of winning the war in Indochina," and that the best for which the French could hope was a stalemate. In the face of the Viet Minh's move into Laos, Navarre decided that the best course of action was the creation of centers of resistance, or "hedgehogs," in locations which threatened the Viet Minh's lines of communication and freedom of movement: the Communist forces would have to attack such hedgehogs, which could be supplied by air, and use their heavier weapons to inflict decisive defeats on the Viet Minh. Navarre selected Dien Bien Phu, which is about 10 miles (16km) north of the Laotian border with

Vietnam and some 175 miles (280km) to the west of Hanoi, as the site of the hedgehog which would best block the Viet Minh from invading Laos.

Dien Bien Phu seemed to offer the French a number of positive features: it lay on the Viet Minh's line of communication into Laos along the Nam Yum river; it already possessed an airstrip, built in the late 1930s and improved by the Japanese to allow supplies to be delivered by air; and it lay in the hills where the Tai tribesmen, loyal to the French, were an active force with whom the Viet Minh would have to cope. Operation Castor was

launched on November 20, 1953 as 1,800 men of the French 1st and 2nd Parachute Battalions dropped into the valley and swiftly eliminated the small Viet Minh garrison.

The French airborne force thus found itself in control of a valley 12 miles (19km) long and 8 miles (13 km) wide, surrounded by heavily-wooded hills. French and Tai units, operating from Lai Chau to the north, swept through the hills and encountered no Viet Minh opposition, leading the French to judge Castor a major tactical success. Giap appreciated that the French position had weaknesses,

however, and began to shift a sizeable proportion of his strength from the De Lattre Line toward Dien Bien Phu. This move was achieved so rapidly that, by the middle of December, the French and Tai patrols in the hills around the small river-valley town were suffering losses so heavy in the course of Communist ambushes that the patrol effort was called off.

The 57-day battle for Dien Bien Phu was to become the longest and hardest-fought by France in its attempt to retain, or rather regain, control of Indochina. The battle began on March 13 with a surprise assault from Communist forces supported, for the first time in the First Indochina War, by heavy artillery as well as large concentrations of antiaircraft artillery. The French plan had been conceived in ignorance of the Viet Minh's possession of such weapons, which soon severed the French lines of communication into the valley by land, as the heavy artillery was sited mostly on the reverse slopes of the flanking hills or otherwise in very carefully concealed positions on the forward slopes. It was soon also severed by air as the airstrip was destroyed, and transport aircraft proved hugely vulnerable to the massed antiaircraft guns, as they attempted to operate from the remnants of the airfield and later to make parachute drops from altitudes low enough to avoid supplies drifting off into Communist-held areas. The French position quickly became untenable, particularly when the advent of the monsoons made the dropping of supplies and reinforcements considerably more difficult.

**OPPOSITE**. A cameraman and other civilians crouch behind armored vehicles in Saigon during the November 1, 1963 coup led by the military on the presidential palace. It resulted in the overthrow and subsequent death of Ngo Dinh Diem, the first president of South Vietnam. This picture was taken by an Associated Press staff photographer.

**RIGHT:** Vietnamese commando troops patrol through swamp territory near Tonkin as they fight the Viet Minh Communist guerrilla forces, using their own game of hit-and-run. French forces had also found commando groups more effective in this area. The man in the lead carries a rifle with an attachment for throwing grenades.

Facing imminent defeat at Dien Bien Phu, the French decided to fight on, despite high losses, and hold Dien Bien Phu as a bargaining counter in the peace conference scheduled to begin in Geneva on April 26. The French made a final break-out of their shrinking perimeter on May 4, which achieved no useful result. The Viet Minh then began to close on the exhausted French, whose ordeal was compounded by the arrival of yet another weapon new to the First Indochina War, namely the Katyusha surface-to-surface artillery rocket, supplied by the Soviets via the Chinese. The Viet Minh's final defeat of the French outpost lasted for two days, from May 6–7, when the French were finally overrun by a frontal assault. General René Cogny, based in Hanoi and commanding the French

forces in northern Vietnam, ordered General Christian de Castries, commanding at Dien Bien Phu, to surrender at 5:30pm, after destroying all matériel to prevent its later use by the Viet Minh. In one of the oddities with which military history abounds, de Castries was also instructed not to use a white flag, so that the ending of hostilities could be treated not as a surrender but as a cease-fire.

The fighting died away on May 7 except in "Isabelle," the isolated southern position of the French defense, where the battle ended at 1:00am on May 8. At least 2,200 of the 20,000-strong French force had been killed or had died during the battle, while the Communist forces of about 100,000 men suffered losses estimated at 8,000 killed and 15,000 wounded. The number of French prisoners taken at Dien Bien Phu was the largest so far achieved by the Viet

Minh, totalling about one-third of all the men taken during the war.

Negotiations between France and the Viet Minh had begun in Geneva during April 1954. Pierre Mendès-France, who had been an opponent of the war since 1950, became prime minister on June 17 on a manifesto of ending the war, with an armistice to be agreed within four months. In fact, agreement was reached on July 21 in the so-called Geneva Accords, which included, among other things, the recognition of the 17th parallel as a "provisional military demarcation line," marking the temporary division of Vietnam into a Communist North Vietnam and pro-Western South Vietnam. The accords also called for free and universal elections during 1956, to select a government for the whole of Vietnam, but the USA and the State of Vietnam refused to sign the document. The Emperor Bao Dai,

**ABOVE:** French personnel stream into the huge belly of a USAF Douglas C-124 Globemaster at Orly airfield, France, for their 8,500-mile (13680-km) air journey to Indochina. The airlift, the largest in aviation history, was directed by the USAF in Europe with aircraft flown from the United States of America.

**OPPOSITE:** The Viet Minh "parade of victory" through the streets of Hanoi, it being the main force of troops to take up occupation in this capital and headquarters city. Approximately 5,000 troops marched or drove vehicles along the streets choked with thousands of Vietnamese civilians cheering them on. Many of the civilians rushed out to present flowers to the marching soldiers, while small children with peace flags waved them on poles above the crowds.

who now lived in France, appointed Ngo Dinh Diem as the prime minister of South Vietnam and in 1955, with U.S. support, Diem used a referendum to remove the emperor and declare himself president of the Republic of Vietnam.

When the elections were prevented by the USA and South Vietnam, Viet Minh cadres in South Vietnam were activated, beginning a campaign of terrorism against the government. North Vietnam invaded and occupied portions of Laos to facilitate their effort to supply the guerrilla and irregular forces of the National Liberation Front in South Vietnam, setting in motion the slide toward the Second Indochina War.

## Text-Dependent Questions

1. What neighboring countries to Vietnam became embroiled in the war?

2. Who led the Viet Minh?

3. When did the First Indochina War begin?

## Research Projects

Summarize the history of the Viet Minh and explain why it was formed.

## Chapter Two
# THE USA BECOMES EMBROILED

It is necessary to backtrack a little here, to explain the steadily increasing U.S. involvement in the First Indochina War, an effort which had included, by 1954, funding some 8 percent of the French war effort. In 1950 the Democratic Republic of Vietnam and China had exchanged mutual recognition, and the USSR followed. President Truman responded by recognizing the government of Vietnam, despite the fact that it was merely a French puppet regime. This

## Words to Understand

**Matériel:** Supplies and equipment, used by an organization.

**Propaganda:** The spread of ideas and information deliberately to further or damage a cause.

**Puppet Regime:** A government controlled by another country's government.

**OPPOSITE:** The helicopter became an effective weapon of war in Vietnam. These are Piasecki H-21 "Flying Banana" twin-rotor helicopters, seen early in the conflict as the USA began to provide matériel aid to the South Vietnamese.

**ABOVE:** The Vietnam People's Army (VPA), not to be confused with the Viet Cong (NLF), was the official name of the armed forces of the Socialist Republic of Vietnam. During the Vietnam War (1957–1975), the U.S. referred to it as the North Vietnamese Army (NVA) or People's Army of Vietnam (PAVN), terms commonly used when speaking of the Vietnam War.

was tacit confirmation that the USA feared the Communist administration in Hanoi was just a tool of a China which was now ruled by the Communists, and by extension, therefore, a tool of the USSR. This was not in fact the case, and there remained strong historically based antipathies between Vietnam and China; but even so, China was willing to provide large quantities of **matériel** and to support the Vietnamese Communists to the end of the war. Another significant factor in 1950, as far as the USA was concerned, was the start of the Korean War (1950–53), for it led to the general belief in U.S. political circles that the First Indochina War should no longer be seen only as a colonial war in

Indochina, but still another element in a program of Communist expansionism controlled by the USSR.

Thus it was during 1950 that the U.S. Military Assistance and Advisory Group (MAAG) arrived to check French requests for equipment, provide advice on strategic matters, and help in the training of Vietnamese soldiers. By 1954 the USA had delivered some 300,000 small arms and had supported the French effort to the tune of US$1 billion.

For the French, their defeat at Dien Bien Phu marked the end of their attempt to regain control of Indochina; at the Geneva Conference the French negotiated a cease-fire agreement, and granted independence to Cambodia, Laos, and Vietnam. Together with the temporary partitioning of Vietnam along the 17th parallel, the Geneva Accords mandated the freedom of civilians to move between the two provisional states, as a result of which nearly a million people, most of them Roman Catholics, moved from the north to the south in fear of the new regime headed by Ho; at the same time it is believed that another two million were forcibly prevented from moving to the south. The Viet Minh established the Democratic Republic of Vietnam as a

**ABOVE and OPPOSITE:** Units of the Vietnamese People's Army, fording a river on their way to the front.

socialist state in the north and embarked on a program of land reform in which very large numbers of "class enemies" were put to death, an error for which Ho later apologized.

Meanwhile, a non-Communist state was established in the south, ruled by the Emperor Bao Dai with Ngo Dinh Diem as prime minister. As many as 90,000 Viet Minh fighters went north for "regroupment," as agreed in the Geneva Accords, but the Viet Minh, in direct contravention of the agreements, and having clearly appreciated the probable course of future events, left behind in South Vietnam some 5,000 to 10,000 cadres as the basis of later political and military operations to take control of South Vietnam.

As ordained by the Geneva Accords, the partition of Vietnam was designed as a temporary measure until the national elections scheduled for July 20, 1956 took place. The partition agreement had also stipulated the creation of a demilitarized zone

(DMZ) along the 17th parallel to keep both North and South Vietnam separated and free from the threat of military action. As noted above, however, the USA was the only major power not to have signed the Geneva Accords, and without U.S. support Diem refused to entertain the holding of the election. President Dwight D. Eisenhower later stated that in 1954 some 80 percent of the population would have voted for the Communist Ho Chi Minh over Bao Dai, but this may not have been the case in the aftermath of the bloody and very unpopular land reform program, and a peasant revolt which was

quashed only with a major loss of life.

Despite its long-stated belief in the concept of democracy, the USA agreed with Diem that democratic elections could not be risked, its reasoning based on the current "domino theory," which suggested that the loss of South Vietnam to Communism would trigger a succession of losses ending with Communist domination of the whole of South-East Asia and, according to the wildest exponents of the theory, a further spread to the Hawaiian Islands and thence to the western seaboard of continental USA. According to the proponents of the

**OPPOSITE:** Air America was the CIA's "airline" in South-East Asia, and is here represented by a Curtiss C-46 Commando twin-engined transport.

**ABOVE:** Council of a National Front for the Liberation of South Vietnam (NLF) or Viet Cong partisan unit in South Vietnam.

domino theory, the spread of Communism had to be tackled sooner rather than later, and the best place to start this process was in South-East Asia rather than any part of the USA. Thus it was a powerful argument for the adoption of South Vietnam as a client state.

The USA's political and military thinking in this respect was based on the concept of containment and, on the basis of the North Atlantic

Treaty Organization, a South-East Asia Treaty Organization (SEATO) was created to co-ordinate the defense of Europe and counter Communist expansion in the region.

Diem, the leader of South Vietnam as agreed by the USA, was a Roman Catholic, strongly anti-Communist, and free of any connection with the French. However, in its ignorance of the reality of South-East Asian affairs,

the USA failed to appreciate that Diem was also an autocrat, a believer in nepotism, and extremely narrow in his nationalism. The Americans also made the major error of looking at the Vietnamese through American eyes, and therefore ascribed American motives to what were uniquely Vietnamese actions. Diem, in fact, warned the Americans of the fallaciousness of their concept and the futility of believing that a Vietnamese emulation of American methods, without thought or "translation" into more appropriate local forms, would or even could solve Vietnamese problems.

Against U.S. advice, Diem decided to simplify and consolidate his own position by removing opposition forces, as he perceived them, through the use of the military: operations were therefore undertaken between April and June 1955 against the Cao Dai religious sect, the Buddhists of the Hoa Hao, and the Binh Xuyen criminal organization, this last being associated with elements of the secret police and some parts of the military establishment. The pretext used by Diem to justify these actions was that the targeted groups protected Communist agents. The ruthless nature of Diem's administration resulted in a broadening of the opposition to it, to which Diem responded by laying the blame on the Communists. From the summer of 1955 Diem initiated a "denounce the Communists" campaign, paving the way for the arrest, imprisonment, torture, and murder, not only of Communists but also of large segments of the opposition to his rule, the latter being classified as Viet

**OPPOSITE:** A Viet Cong prisoner of war, captured by the Army of the Republic of Vietnam (ARVN).

Cong to remove all credibility from their claims to be nationalists.

The movement of refugees continued during this period, some 52,000 civilians moving from south to north, and up to 450,000 others, primarily Catholics, moving from north to south, most of them in French and U.S. aircraft and ships.

Diem next called for a referendum on the future of the monarchy. This was controlled by Diem's brother, Ngo Dinh Nhu, in which it was claimed that 98.2 percent of the vote had gone to Diem when, conscious that the referendum would be rigged, U.S. advisers of the period had recommended that Diem should limit himself to a winning margin of 60 to 70 percent. On October 26, 1955 Diem declared the new Republic of Vietnam, with himself as president, which reflected not only Diem's own ambitions but also the wish of the Eisenhower administration for the creation of a dedicated anti-Communist state within South-East Asia. What the USA ignored, wilfully or in ignorance, was that Diem was already widely distrusted in South Vietnam as a wealthy Catholic who "must have had" a cosy relationship within the minority which aided the French to rule Vietnam, as a man opposed to the majority Buddhist beliefs of the region, and as one who was trampling on all manner of human rights.

In 1956 Le Duan, one of the leading Communists in the south, traveled to the north and recommended that a more determined stance be taken in the struggle to ensure that Vietnam was reunited under Communist rule. The problem for North Vietnam was that it was currently facing acute domestic problems because of its collapsed economy, and did not feel the time to be ripe for any large-scale military endeavor. North Vietnam feared U.S.

intervention at this stage, and also felt South Vietnamese conditions to be currently unsuitable for any "people's revolution." The overall objective, nonetheless, remained the reunification of Vietnam under Communist rule, and in December 1956 Ho Chi Minh ordered the Viet Minh cadres in South Vietnam to begin a low-intensity insurgency. This "armed propaganda," as it was termed, took the form mostly of kidnappings and terrorist attacks. Some 400 members of the South Vietnamese administration were murdered in 1957, and the pace of this low-level violence was steadily increased from local government officials to many elements of South Vietnamese society, such as teachers, health workers, and agricultural officers: it is estimated that by 1958, 20 percent of South Vietnam's village chiefs may have been murdered as part of this Communist effort, which was directed at the destabilization if not complete destruction of government control in South Vietnam's rural areas, so that a National Liberation Front shadow administration could be emplaced.

During January 1959, as a result of pressure from South Vietnamese cadres being increasingly targeted by the secret police, the Central Committee in North Vietnam promulgated to the cadres a secret resolution calling for the "armed struggle" phase of the program to take over South Vietnam. This phase was based on the launch of large-scale operations against the South Vietnamese military. Diem countered this with still stronger anti-Communist legislation, which was inadequate to prevent the increasing supply by North Vietnam of troops and supplies; the infiltration of still more men and weapons passed from North to South Vietnam via the many secret channels of the "Ho Chi Minh Trail" through neutral Laos and

Cambodia, thereby bypassing the DMZ and avoiding the need, at this stage, to attempt major movements by sea where, with US support, South Vietnam was considerably stronger.

On December 12, 1960, the increasing level of South Vietnamese detestation of the corrupt Diem administration persuaded North Vietnam that the time was right for the creation of the National Front for the Liberation of South Vietnam (NLF), comprising nationalist and Communist groupings, although the latter had overall political control and steadily subsumed or eliminated the former. The task of the NLF was not overtly military, but covertly political, with the object of securing political control of South Vietnam by means of

a popular rising. The key elements in the NLF's overall message, much boosted by a carefully orchestrated propaganda campaign, were patriotism, political and personal honesty, good government, the reunification of Vietnam, and the expulsion of U.S. influences.

U.S. administrations right through the period before and during the Vietnam War believed firmly but wrongly that North Vietnam exercised a monolithic control over the NLF, and thereby played down the extent to which the population of South Vietnam was being progressively alienated and angered by the repression and incompetence of Diem's paranoid administration. But it would be wrong to suggest that the

NLF reflected an exclusively South Vietnamese reaction to Diem's rule, when, right from the start, North Vietnam had exploited any anti-Diem/anti-U.S. feelings in South Vietnam for its own ends.

During June 1961, only five months after his inauguration, President John F. Kennedy met Soviet premier Nikita Khrushchev in Vienna to discuss US/Soviet issues, but were unable to effect a significant rapport. In these circumstances, the U.S. strategists and analysts of the period believed that South-East Asia would rapidly become the region in which Soviet forces would test the validity of the USA's policy of containment, which had been adopted somewhat tentatively in the course of the

Ho Chi Minh, famous for leading the Viet Minh independence movement from 1941 onward. He established the Communist-governed Democratic Republic of Vietnam in 1945, defeating the French Union in 1954 at Dien Bien Phu. He led the North Vietnamese in the Vietnam War until his death in 1969, the war ending six years later with a North Vietnamese victory, with Vietnamese unification following on. Saigon, the former capital of South Vietnam, was renamed Ho Chi Minh City in his honor.

Truman administration, and had become solidified, almost into dogma, as a result of the Korean War during the Eisenhower administration. The linchpin of the Kennedy administration's military policy was a U.S. parity in long-range missile capability with the Soviets, but Kennedy was also a believer in the use of high-grade special forces, backed by the full extent of U.S. technology

**OPPOSITE:** Entry of victorious Vietnamese People's Army troops into Ha Long (Hong Gai) in April 1955.

**ABOVE:** "One of three North Vietnamese torpedo boats are shown in an attack on the destroyer USS Maddox," reads the caption to this photograph, released by the U.S. Defense Department shortly after the incident of August 2, 1964 took place in the Gulf of Tonkin.

and intelligence capabilities, to undertake successful operations in Third World countries to defeat the threat of Communist insurgencies. Kennedy believed that the tactics of low-intensity warfare, employed by special forces such as the Green Berets, would be effective in a "police action" campaign in Vietnam. Kennedy's beliefs, it should be noted, were based on the successful use of the tactics by the British to defeat the Communists in the Malayan Emergency (1948–60).

The year 1961 also saw the Kennedy administration faced with a trio of crises (the failure of the "Bay of Pigs" invasion of Cuba, the construction of the Berlin Wall separating the Communist East Berlin from the three Western enclaves in the city's western part, and the settlement between the pro-Western government of Laos and the Communist Pathet Lao forces) and Kennedy himself

came to believe that another US failure to check Communist expansion would seriously undermine the credibility of the USA with its allies. For these and other, sometimes personal reasons, Kennedy decided that Communism had to be checked in Vietnam. In May 1961 Vice-President Lyndon B. Johnson visited Saigon and told Diem that he could rely on more US aid to allow the development of a South Vietnamese military capability able to defeat the Communists.

**LEFT:** The bodies of Dang Van Bay and Phan Van Tro, killed by the Viet Cong at 7:30pm on October 13, 1960, in Hoa Hiep Hamlet, Go Cong District.

**BELOW:** Sgt Howard A. Stevens, an adviser from the 77th Ranger Detachment, conducting a class on the care and cleaning of the M-1 rifle in 1962.

**OPPOSITE:** A helicopter of the U.S. Marine Helicopter Squadron 92 passes over a lonely outpost in the guerrilla-infested mountain area of north-central Vietnam in 1963.

Throughout this apparently inexorable drift of the USA toward direct involvement in Vietnam, albeit only in an advisory capacity, Kennedy remained convinced that the solution had to be based on the defeat of the Communist irregular forces within South Vietnam by South Vietnamese forces, and initially refused to consider the deployment of U.S. ground forces.

The trouble with this U.S. perception, however, was that the South Vietnamese armed forces were qualitatively poor, largely as a result of inadequate leadership by officers concerned with promoting their own interests rather than those of their men, corruption which robbed the men of their pay and the equipment they needed, and political interference which promoted Diem's adherents over all others. Thus the Army of the Republic of Vietnam (ARVN) was incapable of the tasks demanded of it, not only for the reasons listed above, but also as a result of the dismally poor morale stemming from the situation. In these circumstances the Communist irregular forces were able to raise the tempo of their attacks as the insurgency gathered momentum in the military vacuum provided by the ARVN's incapacity. American analysts suggested that some of the burden should be assumed by U.S. troops, landed in South Vietnam in the guise of flood relief workers, and while Kennedy rejected the notion, he did authorize a further increase in military assistance, despite the warnings of several influential thinkers and analysts. By the middle of 1962, the original force of 700 military advisers in South Vietnam had swollen to a strength of 12,000.

By this time the Strategic Hamlet Program, schemed by South Vietnamese and US officials, had

**OPPOSITE:** Newly-arrived trainees sign for equipment from supplies at a Civil Defense Group training camp in Thua Thien Hue province. July 1963.

**ABOVE:** Sfc Johnny F. Cooper instructs a group of Montagnard tribesmen in the use of a 60-mm mortar in 1963. Language being one of the main problems, an interpreter kneels to Cooper's left, translating from English to Vietnamese, while standing behind is another, who then translates the Vietnamese language into one of many Montagnard tribal dialects.

already begun. The object of this was to combat the Communist-led insurgency through the movement of populations which might otherwise fall under Communist influence or control. In 1961, therefore, U.S. advisers launched a major effort to isolate peasant communities in the South Vietnamese countryside from contact with, and therefore influence by, the NLF. Together with its smaller-scale predecessor, the Rural Community Development Program, the Strategic Hamlet Program was of great significance in setting the course of South Vietnamese events in the late

1950s and early 1960s. The two programs were akin to each other in seeking to ensure the separation of peasant communities from Communist irregular and insurgent forces through the establishment of fortified villages, and also by forcing the peasants to take an active role in what was, in effect, a civil war. The communities targeted in the Strategic Hamlet Program were of great importance to the Communist forces: together with tactics such as assassination, sabotage, and sneak attacks on government troops, the irregular forces and guerrillas saw the obvious political as

well as military advantages of winning the support of the peasant communities, which could thus supply recruits, shelter, food, and, perhaps most importantly, current information. The adherence of South Vietnam's civil population, moreover, was in effect the touchstone of eventual success. Thus the Communists sought to win the rural communities over by propaganda, co-operation, and when these failed, coercion.

From 1954 or thereabouts, the South Vietnamese authorities had been coming down with an increasingly heavy hand on those whom it believed to be Communists or Communist sympathizers. All this achieved, in reality, was a further alienation of rural communities already disaffected by the greater wealth of urban communities, which they saw as the origins of all governmental evils. Soon after its formation in 1959, the NLF had built up what was, in effect, almost total control over large sections of rural South Vietnam, at a time when there were only about 10,000 insurgents in the whole of South Vietnam. Diem and his brother recognized the threat that was being posed and launched the Rural Community Development Program (later "Agroville") in the same year. Based in part on the success of a comparable effort by the British in Malaya, the Agroville concept attempted to isolate rural communities from contact with the Communist irregulars. Both incentive and force were employed in a "carrot and stick" approach to uproot typical

History of the Vietnam War 1947–1975 Map

**OPPOSITE ABOVE:** Troops of a US 8th Airborne Battalion unload from a H-21 Shawnee helicopter to begin a mission. December 1962.

**ABOVE:** U.S. adviser Captain Linton Beasley and Vietnamese 1st Lt Nguyen Tien inspect the weapons of a Vietnamese platoon during a training exercise. The U.S. forces were in South Vietnam at that time as advisers and instructors, and to assist South Vietnam in matters of training, logistics, communications, and transportation. They were under instructions not to fire unless fired upon. May 1962.

small rural communities for relocation into larger Agroville communities, with the result that some 23 of these, each with a population of several thousands, had been built by 1960.

This was, in effect, a forced migration, in that the obvious error had been made of separating the peasants from land which may have been in their families for many generations; when the peasant population demanded a reconsideration of the policy it was seen as playing right into the hands of the Communists. During 1961 the South Vietnamese government, with the aid of a number of U.S. advisers, attempted to reshape the Agroville concept into what then became the Strategic Hamlet Program. This was based on smaller communities, each with fewer than 1,000 inhabitants, created on existing and also newly-developed settlements. Each of the hamlets was to be heavily fortified, relying for its defense on its own inhabitants supported by patrol forces as and when required. Each hamlet would have its own radio equipment for external communications, the arrangements for the hamlets also including supply lines, medical treatment, and improved education facilities. In practice, few of these ever materialized.

South Vietnam was trying to accomplish too much too quickly when it began the Strategic Hamlet Program. In September 1962, the USA noted, 4.3 million people had been moved to 3,225 completed hamlets and another 2,000 or more were being developed; by July 1963 more than 8.5 million people had been settled in 7,205 hamlets. Thus in less than 12 months the number of completed hamlets and their populations had doubled, and this made it impossible for the South Vietnamese authorities either to support or protect the hamlets and their populations, despite the huge amounts of money being poured into the program by the USA. As a result, the insurgents were finding it easier to sabotage and overrun these poorly defended communities, and so gained the access they required to the South Vietnamese peasantry. It is estimated that something in the order of 80 percent of the hamlets in the heavily populated delta of the great Mekong river were under the control of the insurgents by the end of 1963.

The NLF, now increasingly known as the Viet Cong, capitalized on the general unpopularity of the

Strategic Hamlets Program to launch its own program of clever propaganda, which further exacerbated the peasant population's anger towards the South Vietnamese government. Few of the hamlet locations were both safe and possessed of good land; some peasants were forced to walk longer distances each day between their accommodation and the rice paddies, while others had been forced to leave the graves of their ancestors, or were compelled to work without payment to build the defenses of their hamlets.

Coupled with the rising hatred for Diem, and his family, who controlled the program and refused to listen to any complaint, the Strategic Hamlet Program was almost inevitably a failure, and in fact collapsed with the assassination of Diem late in 1963, the dissolution of the Committee for Strategic Hamlets occurring early in the following year.

One particular event early in January 1963 provided the USA with striking evidence that the Diem administration's earlier "successes" against the Viet Cong were either illusory or the result of natural events rather than any real military capability by the South Vietnamese army. Right at the beginning of 1963, South Vietnamese intelligence had discovered that a Viet Cong radio station was in operation close to the village of Ap Bac in the Plain of Reeds, estimating that the installation was being guarded only by a small force of irregulars. This seemed to be the opportunity for an easy victory, so the South Vietnamese command immediately dispatched a multi-battalion force composed of infantry, ranger (commando), helicopter, and armored units, supported by 51 U.S. military advisers.

Almost everything that could go wrong did in fact go awry in the battle which followed on January 2. Instead

of encountering a company of irregulars, the South Vietnamese army force arrived at Ap Bac to face the Viet Cong 514th Battalion, a highly capable unit of some 400 regulars. Five U.S. helicopters supporting the operation were destroyed within a few minutes: two succumbed to ground fire, one to an engine failure, and two after their pilots flew into the line of fire of the Viet Cong's weapons, in an attempt to rescue downed comrades who were, in fact, already safe behind friendly lines. As the fighting developed, the U.S. advisers suggested the South Vietnamese, who had the benefit of a considerable superiority in numbers and firepower, should advance, but the South Vietnamese commanders (none of them above a captain, field-grade officers considering themselves too important to be risked in field service) were fully aware of Diem's feelings that casualties threatened his own position. The South Vietnamese officers procrastinated, one taking almost four hours to advance his armored personnel carriers a mere 1,500 yards (1370m) in the face of Viet Cong small arms fire that was incapable of penetrating the vehicles' protection. When the U.S. advisers called for an airborne drop east of Ap Bac, to cut the Viet Cong's line of escape, the airborne troopers were in fact dropped to the west of the village and were therefore wholly wasted. When the U.S. advisers called for a heavy artillery barrage, the South Vietnamese artillery responded with a mere four rounds per hour. The Viet

Vietnam War: History and Key Dates

Cong, therefore, were able to escape under cover of darkness, but not before a South Vietnamese air attack had inadvertently struck a friendly unit, causing many casualties. Reliable sources report that besides the five helicopters destroyed, 11 more were damaged, and 65 South Vietnamese troops were killed, together with three U.S. advisers. The wounded totaled about 100 South Vietnamese and six Americans.

American reporters knew nothing of the battle at the time of its start,

**ABOVE:** A U.S. Army adviser accompanies Vietnamese rangers in the Mekong river delta area in July 1962.

**OPPOSITE:** A base camp in the Vietnamese Highlands used by Communist irregular forces.

but arrived shortly after it had ended and recorded the angry assessment of the U.S. advisers concerning the performance of the South Vietnamese. One correspondent "managed to overhear" a confidential briefing for General Paul D. Harkins, commanding the MACV, and other correspondents were in the area on

January 3 when, in the course of mopping-up operations, South Vietnam artillery accidentally bombarded its own men. In these circumstances, therefore, the journalists had more than enough evidence to validate the most pessimistic estimations that they had already began to formulate.

The reports that appeared in U.S. newspapers led to a considerable outcry against Diem within the USA. American commentators were able to show that the USA had spent US$400 million on South Vietnam and that 50 U.S. service personnel had been killed while Diem steadfastly refuse to implement the program of reform he

**ABOVE:** Ban Me Thout, the capital of Dak Lak province, Vietnam. M/Sgt John M. Stover, 1st Special Forces, Company A, Okinawa, returning from patrol with Rhade volunteers. 1962.

had promised to make in exchange for U.S. aid. Meanwhile, the Communist irregular forces were enjoying what was in effect a free run of South Vietnam's rural areas, and South Vietnamese officers were unwilling to commit their forces to combat even with the advantages of numbers and firepower. The only thing the USA could do in the circumstances, many

commentators demanded, was to take full control of the war.

U.S. officials in Washington and Saigon attempted to reassure Diem that they supported him despite the adverse press reports, but Diem still refused to implement the reforms that were manifestly required and had indeed been promised. The U.S. attempt to shield and protect Diem only made matters worse. When representatives of the Department of State claimed that the South Vietnamese had fought with "courage and determination" at Ap Bac, and both Harkins and Admiral Harry D. Felt, the commander-in-chief Pacific,

stated that the battle had been a victory for the South Vietnamese, some U.S. newspapers retorted that the situation in South Vietnam must indeed be critical if the U.S. policy of loyalty to the Diem administration demanded the dissemination of "such thin and unconvincing whitewash." The Ap Bac episode further divided all levels of U.S. representation in South Vietnam. So annoyed were they by the adverse press reports, that senior officials at the U.S. Embassy limited their contacts with journalists to formal occasions, and set about putting the best face possible on the course of events on the ground. The

**ABOVE:** An American soldier scrambles to escape from a burning helicopter recently crashed in the Communist-held Ca Mau area, on the southern tip of South Vietnam. The troop-carrying U.S. helicopter was taking part, with other aircraft, in an operation over the area when it crashed. After all on board had been transferred to other aircraft, the helicopter was destroyed to prevent it from falling into enemy hands.

converse of this approach, however, was that the U.S. journalistic corps began to look at events in South Vietnam with increasingly jaundiced eyes, emphasizing and on occasion exaggerating everything they felt was wrong.

Of course, the South Vietnamese could have silenced the growing level of journalistic criticism by securing military success, or at least starting the program of military reforms which the USA had demanded, but Diem attempted neither and allowed the course of events merely to drift.

At this stage of the conflict it was in the interests of all, including the

Communists, that the conflict be limited to Vietnam, and on July 23, 1962 some 14 countries, including China, North Vietnam, South Vietnam, the USA, and the USSR reached an agreement promising the neutrality of Laos.

By this time the U.S. administration had become wholly exasperated with Diem, and it was the belief of some analysts that he might even be preparing to reach a political accommodation with Ho Chi Minh, being more concerned with preserving his own position than prosecuting the war. In the course of the summer of 1963, therefore, there was discussion

certain impossibility of persuading Diem to remove his brother, and this, in effect, sealed Diem's own fate.

The year was also marked by an altogether heavy-handed crackdown on Buddhist monks protesting about the Diem administration's discriminatory practices, and demanding their voice be heard in political circles. Diem's suppression of the protests by force triggered the "Buddhist Revolt," in which several monks doused themselves in petrol before setting fire to themselves as they sat placidly on the road. Several of these self-immolations were seen and recorded by the press for broadcast all over the world, leading to a wave of revulsion for the Diem administration. The Communist propaganda system exploited the situation for all it was worth, causing anti-Diem feelings to harden to destabilize South Vietnam's internal situation still further.

The CIA had already established links with South Vietnamese generals plotting the removal of Diem, and passed on the information that the USA would support any such move, even though the matter had not even been raised with the president. Diem was overthrown, and the two brothers were executed on November 2, 1963. The immediate consequence of the

**LEFT:** A South Vietnamese soldier questions a villager during an anti-Viet Cong patrol.

**OPPOSITE:** Captain Robert L. Webster, from Falls Church, Virginia, a pilot of one of the newly arrived UH-1B helicopters of the Utility Tactical Transport Helicopter Company, Saigon, examines MXL Emerson Squad 4 machine guns, mounted on his UH-1B, and operated by remote control by the co-pilot. December 1962.

concerning the possibility of "regime change" in South Vietnam, but although the U.S. Department of State was in favor of encouraging a coup against Diem, the Department of Defense and the Central Intelligence Agency each warned that this might be even more destabilizing than leaving Diem in place under increasing U.S. pressure. Among the many suggestions as to the ways in which matters in South Vietnam might be improved was the removal of Diem's brother, Ngo Dinh Nhu, who headed the secret police and was widely perceived as the force behind the suppression of the Buddhists. But the USA appreciated the almost

coup was total disorder in South Vietnam, a fact which North Vietnam immediately exploited to boost the level of support it was providing to the insurgents, who now had a freer hand as South Vietnam passed into a period of great political instability: military administrations followed each other in short order, and the approval of the South Vietnamese for their government fell steadily as the military came to be seen as little more than a puppet of the USA.

The rapid rise in the level and pace of the Communist insurgency persuaded Kennedy to authorize the dispatch of still more advisers to South Vietnam, the ultimate figure being 16,300 to cope with rising guerrilla activity. These advisers were allocated to every level of the South Vietnamese military establishment, but whatever their competence at the purely military level, they lacked all but the most rudimentary appreciation, if even that, of the political situation, which was all-important in understanding the nature of the conflict being waged in South Vietnam. At the political level in the USA there was a greater understanding that the insurgency was a political power struggle, and the Kennedy administration was switching to a policy with its eyes on pacification and success in the "hearts and minds" campaign intended to win the support of South Vietnam's population. But despite the warnings of the CIA, which highlighted the insurgency's control of much of South Vietnam's countryside, the Department of Defense remained convinced that the advisers should continue to be used only for training troops. By this time Kennedy had come to the conclusion that the USA's best course would be to extricate itself from South Vietnam, if only a way could be found to achieve this without the total disintegration of the USA's position and reputation as leader of the "free world."

Kennedy was assassinated on 22 November 1963 and was succeeded by his vice-president, Lyndon B. Johnson, who swiftly reaffirmed U.S. support for South Vietnam. By the end of the year Saigon had received US$500 million in military aid, a large proportion of which was "lost" in the mire of corruption endemic in the South Vietnamese administration. But Johnson allocated higher priority to his "great society" and "social progressive" programs, and thus did not believe in the extreme urgency of the South Vietnamese situation as he took over from Kennedy. This tendency was exacerbated by the fact that Johnson was in essence a "domestic" American and therefore had little understanding of the mindset of U.S. foreign policy-makers, neither did he get on with McGeorge Bundy, the National Security adviser he had inherited from Kennedy. But on November 24, 1963 Johnson brought a small group together to talk with Henry Cabot Lodge, the U.S. ambassador in South Vietnam, and was persuaded to offer his support in winning the Vietnam War. This was a promise hard to make but harder still to implement, even as the situation in South Vietnam was deteriorating rapidly, especially in regions such as the Mekong delta, following the coup which had removed Diem.

The South Vietnamese Military Revolutionary Council, which now ruled the country, had 12 members and was led by Lieutenant General Duong Van Minh, tellingly described as "a model of lethargy." In the first month of 1964, however, Minh's administration was toppled by one led by Major General Nguyen Khanh.

**OPPOSITE:** Vietnamese army personnel training in the jungle.

## Text-Dependent Questions

1. Summarize the main reasons why the USA became embroiled in war in Vietnam.

2. Explain the reasons behind the "Buddhists Revolt."

3. Why did the USA fear the spread of Communism?

## Research Project

Write a biography of Ngo Dinh Diem.

# TIME LINE OF THE VIETNAM WAR

**1858** French colonial rule begins.

**1930** Ho Chi Minh founds the Indochinese Communist Party (ICP).

**1941** ICP organises a guerrilla force, Viet Minh, in response to invasion by Japan during World War II.

**1945** The Viet Minh seizes power. Ho Chi Minh announces Vietnam's independence.

**1946** French forces attack Viet Minh in Haiphong in November, sparking the war of resistance against the colonial power.

**1950** Democratic Republic of Vietnam is recognised by China and USSR.

**1954** Viet Minh forces attack an isolated French military outpost in the town of Dien Bien Phu. The attempt to take the outpost lasts two months, during which time the French government agrees to peace talks in Geneva.

Vietnam is split into North and South at Geneva conference.

**1956** South Vietnamese President Ngo Dinh Diem begins campaign against political dissidents.

**1957** Beginning of Communist insurgency in the South.

**1959** Weapons and men from North Vietnam begin infiltrating the South.

**1960** American aid to Diem increased.

**1962** Number of U.S. military advisors in South Vietnam rises to 12,000.

**1963** Viet Cong, the communist guerrillas operating in South Vietnam, defeat units of the ARVN, the South Vietnamese Army.

President Diem is overthrown and then killed in a U.S.-backed military coup.

## U.S. ENTERS THE WAR

**1964** Gulf of Tonkin incident: the U.S. says North Vietnamese patrol boats fire on two U.S. Navy destroyers. U.S. Congress approves Gulf of Tonkin Resolution, authorising military action in region.

**1965** 200,000 American combat troops arrive in South Vietnam.

**1966** U.S. troop numbers in Vietnam rise to 400,000, then to 500,000 the following year.

**1968** Tet Offensive - a combined assault by Viet Cong and the North Vietnamese army on U.S. positions - begins. More than 500 civilians die in the U.S. massacre at My Lai. Thousands are killed by communist forces during their occupation of the city of Hue.

**1969** Ho Chi Minh dies. President Nixon begins to reduce U.S. ground troops in Vietnam as domestic public opposition to the war grows.

**1970** Nixon's national security advisor, Henry Kissinger, and Le Duc Tho, for the Hanoi government, start talks in Paris.

**1973** Cease-fire agreement in Paris, U.S. troop pull-out completed by March.

**1975** North Vietnamese troops invade South Vietnam and take control of the whole country after South Vietnamese President Duong Van Minh surrenders.

**OPPOSITE:** President Lyndon Johnson awards a medal to a wounded U.S. serviceman in Cam Rahn Bay, South Vietnam.

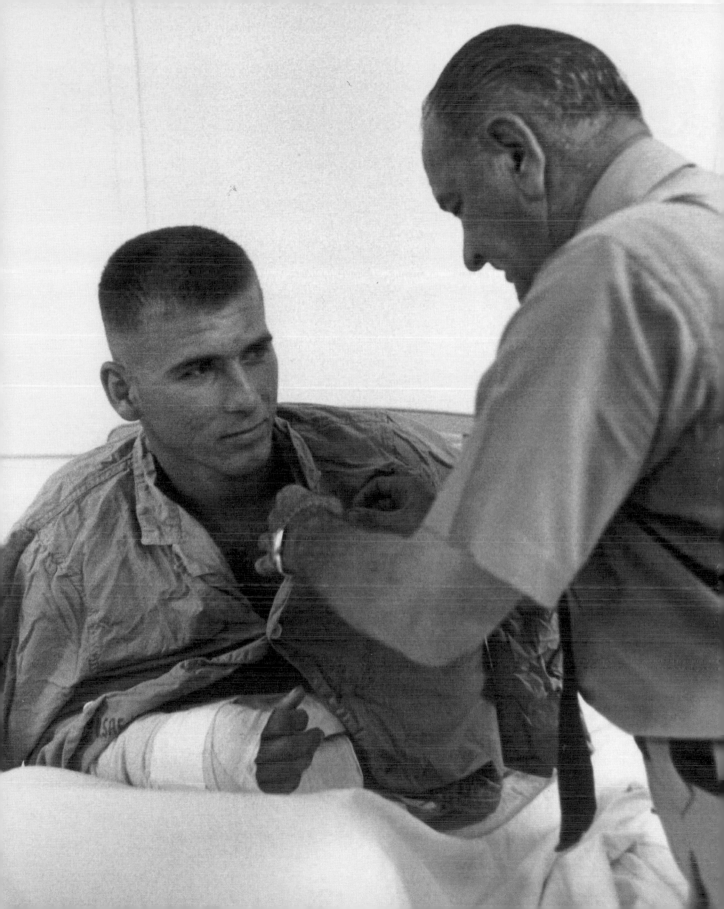

## Series Glossary of Key Terms

**ARVN**  Army of the Republic of Vietnam.

**Boat People**  A term given to refugees fleeing Vietnam following the Communist takeover.

**Body Count**  The number of enemy soldiers killed in an engagement.

**Charlie, Charles** or **Mr Charlie**  Slang for the Viet Cong.

**Chopper**  Helicopter.

**Containment**  U.S. government policy to prevent the spread of Communism.

**Demilitarized Zone (DMZ)**  The line that divided North Vietnam and South Vietnam, located at the 17th parallell.

**Domino Theory** A chain of events describing a situation when one country falls to Communism, others will follow.

**DRV**  Acronym for Democratic Republic of Vietnam.

**Friendly Fire** An accidental attack on one's own military forces.

**Gulf of Tonkin Incident** Two attacks by North Vietnam against U.S. destroyers *USS Maddox* and USS *Turner Joy*.

**Ho Chi Minh Trail** Supply paths used by Communist forces to supply troops fighting in the South.

**Irregulars**  Armed individuals or groups not members of regular armed forces.

**Napalm**  A defoliant chemical dispersed by bombs or flamethrowers, used to destroy foliage in order to expose enemy troops.

**Post-traumatic Stress Disorder**  A psychological disorder caused by experiencing trauma. Symptoms include flashbacks, nightmares, lack of sleep, and other psychological problems.

**POW**  Acronym for prisoner of war.

**MIA**  Acronym for missing in action.

**Tet Offensive**  A large scale attack on South Vietnam by North Vietnam's army and the Viet Cong.

**Tonkin**  Northern section of Vietnam.

**Tunnel Rats**  Soldiers who explored the network of tunnels constructed by the Viet Cong.

**Viet Cong**  Communist guerrilla forces in South Vietnam.

**Viet Minh**  League for the Independence of Vietnam established by Ho Chi Minh.

**Vietnamization** The process of withdrawing U.S. troops from Vietnam and turning over combat to the South Vietnamese.

# Further Reading and Internet Resources

## WEBSITES

http://spartacus-educational.com/VietnamWar.htm

http://www.history.com/topics/vietnam-war

https://www.britannica.com/event/Vietnam-War

http://www.historynet.com/vietnam-war

## BOOKS

Hourly History. *Vietnam War: A History From Beginning to End,* Hourly History Ltd., 2016. Kindle edition 2016.

Mark Atwood Lawrence. *The Vietnam War: A Concise International History.* Oxford University Press, 2010

Stuart Murray. *DK Eyewltness Books: Vietnam War. DK Publishing Inc.*, 2005.

**If you enjoyed this book take a look at Mason Crest's other war series:**

**The Civil War, World War II, Major U.S. Historical Wars.**

**OVERLEAF**

The Vietnam Veterans Memorial is a 2-acre (8,000 m²) national memorial in Washington, D.C. It honors U.S. service members of the U.S. armed forces who fought in the Vietnam War, service members who died in service in Vietnam/South East Asla, and those service members who were unaccounted for (Missing In Action) during the War.

Page numbers in **_bold italics_** refer to photographs and their captions or to videos.

**OPPOSITE**: An infantryman of the 2nd Batallion, 5th Marines.

## PHOTOGRAPHIC ACKNOWLEDGEMENTS

All images in this book are supplied by Cody Images and are in the public domain.

The content of this book was first published as *VIETNAM WAR*.

## ABOUT THE AUTHOR
### Christopher Chant

Christopher Chant is a successful writer on aviation and modern military matters, and has a substantial number of authoritative titles to his credit. He was born in Cheshire, England in December 1945, and spent his childhood in East Africa, where his father was an officer in the Colonial Service. He returned to the UK for his education at the King's School, Canterbury (1959–64) and at Oriel College, Oxford (1964–68). Aviation in particular and military matters in general have long been a passion, and after taking his degree he moved to London as an assistant editor on the Purnell partworks, *History of the Second World War* (1968–69) and *History of the First World War* (1969–72). On completion of the latter he moved to Orbis Publishing as editor of the partwork, *World War II* (1972–74), on completion of which he decided to become a freelance writer and editor.

Living first in London, then in Lincolnshire after his marriage in 1978, and currently in Sutherland, at the north-western tip of Scotland, he has also contributed as editor and writer to the partworks, *The Illustrated Encyclopedia of Aircraft*, *War Machine*, *Warplane*, *Take-Off*, *World Aircraft Information Files* and *World Weapons*, and to the magazine *World Air Power Journal*. In more recent years he was also involved in the creation of a five-disk CR-ROM series, covering the majority of the world's military aircraft from World War I to the present, and also in the writing of scripts for a number of video cassette and TV programs, latterly for Continuo Creative.

As sole author, Chris has more than 90 books to his credit, many of them produced in multiple editions and co-editions, including more than 50 on aviation subjects. As co-author he has contributed to 15 books, ten of which are also connected with aviation. He has written the historical narrative and technical database for a five-disk *History of Warplanes* CD-ROM series, and has been responsible for numerous video cassette programs on military and aviation matters, writing scripts for several TV programmes and an A–Z 'All the World's Aircraft' section in Aerospace/Bright Star *World Aircraft Information Files* partwork. He has been contributing editor to a number of books on naval, military and aviation subjects as well as to numerous partworks concerned with military history and technology. He has also produced several continuity card sets on aircraft for publishers such as Agostini, Del Prado, Eaglemoss, Edito-Service and Osprey.